Creative Crafts for Kids

Costume CRAFTS

By Tessa Brown

Gareth Stevens
Publishing

Please visit our Web site www.garethstevens.com. For a free color catalog of all our high-quality books, call toll free 1-800-542-2595 or fax 1-877-542-2596.

Library of Congress Cataloging-in-Publication Data
Brown, Tessa, 1963-
    Costume crafts / Tessa Brown.
        p. cm. — (Creative crafts for kids)
    Includes index.
    ISBN 978-1-4339-3555-8 (library binding)
    ISBN 978-1-4339-3556-5 (pbk.)
    ISBN 978-1-4339-3557-2 (6-pack)
    1. Costume—Juvenile literature. 2. Handicraft—Juvenile literature. I. Title.
TT633.B78 2010
745.594—dc22   2009041570

Published in 2010 by
Gareth Stevens Publishing
111 East 14th Street, Suite 349
New York, NY 10003

© 2010 The Brown Reference Group Ltd.

For Gareth Stevens Publishing:
Art Direction: Haley Harasymiw
Editorial Direction: Kerri O'Donnell

For The Brown Reference Group Ltd:
Editorial Director: Lindsey Lowe
Managing Editor: Tim Harris
Children's Publisher: Anne O'Daly
Design Manager: David Poole
Production Director: Alastair Gourlay

Picture Credits:
All photographs: Martin Norris
Front Cover: iStock: Viorika and Martin Norris

Manufactured in the United States of America
1 2 3 4 5 6 7 8 9   12 11 10

CPSIA compliance information: Batch #BRW0102GS: For further information contact Gareth Stevens, New York, New York at 1-800-542-2595.

Contents

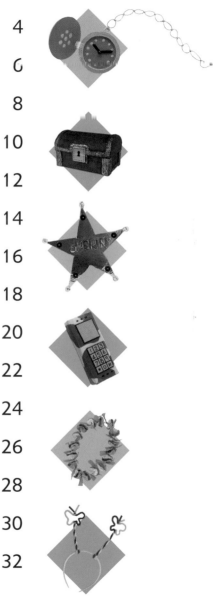

Introduction

If you're dressing up for a play or a party, take a look in this book for some inspiring costume ideas. There are pretty pastel wings for a butterfly, bird, or fairy on page 22 and a parrot that perches on your shoulder on page 26. Use your imagination to adapt the projects to suit your character.

YOU WILL NEED

Each project includes a list of all the things you need.

Before you go out and buy lots of new materials, have a look around at home to see what you could use instead. For example, you can cut cardboard shapes out of old boxes. Save up some foil candy wrappers to make the crown on page 18.

You can buy pipe cleaners, crêpe paper, craft foam, and foam board from a craft shop. You can buy cable for the football helmet and fabrics, such as mock leather and muslin, from a department store.

Getting started

Read the steps for the project first.

Gather together all the items you need.

Cover your work surface with newspaper.

Wear an apron, or change into old clothes.

A message for adults

All the projects in Costume Crafts have been designed for children to make, but occasionally they will need you to help. Some of the projects do require the use of sharp utensils, such as scissors or needles. Please read the instructions before your child starts work.

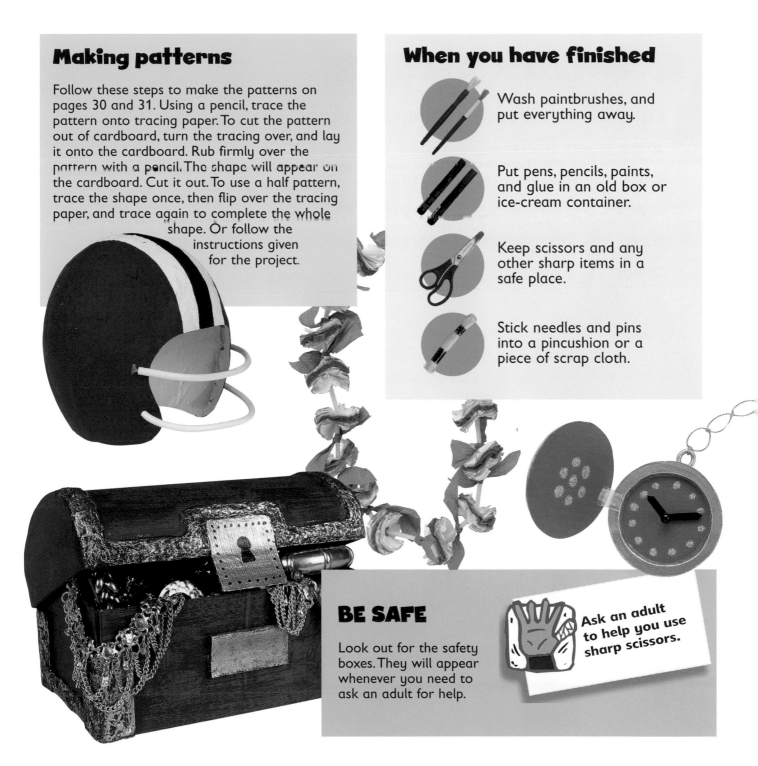

Making patterns

Follow these steps to make the patterns on pages 30 and 31. Using a pencil, trace the pattern onto tracing paper. To cut the pattern out of cardboard, turn the tracing over, and lay it onto the cardboard. Rub firmly over the pattern with a pencil. The shape will appear on the cardboard. Cut it out. To use a half pattern, trace the shape once, then flip over the tracing paper, and trace again to complete the whole shape. Or follow the instructions given for the project.

When you have finished

Wash paintbrushes, and put everything away.

Put pens, pencils, paints, and glue in an old box or ice-cream container.

Keep scissors and any other sharp items in a safe place.

Stick needles and pins into a pincushion or a piece of scrap cloth.

BE SAFE

Look out for the safety boxes. They will appear whenever you need to ask an adult for help.

Ask an adult to help you use sharp scissors.

Cowgirl chaps

Cowgirls and boys wear leather chaps to protect their jeans when they're on horseback. You can make chaps of your own from mock leather or any spare tough fabric.

YOU WILL NEED

two pieces of brown mock leather, each 27in x 22in (68cm x 55cm)

scissors

felt-tip pen

hole punch

large needle

red ribbon or twine

ruler

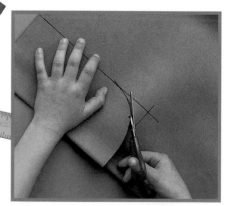

1 To make one leg of the chaps, fold a piece of fabric in half lengthwise with the right side of the fabric facing inward. Draw a rectangle 9in x 4in (23cm x 10cm) in one corner on the fold. Draw a curved corner as shown above.

2 Cut out this rectangle, following the curved corner line. This is where the chaps will curve around your inside leg.

3 Make marks every 1in (2.5cm) along the opposite edge, about ½in (1cm) in from the edge of the fabric. If you are using mock leather fabric, use a hole punch to make holes where you have made marks. If you are using a softer fabric, you can use these marks as a guide for sewing.

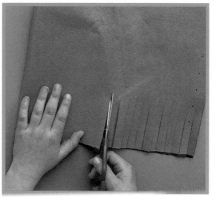

4 Cut a fringe along the bottom edge of the fabric.

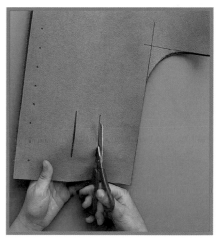

5 At the top of the leg, cut two slits to make belt loops. Cut the slits slightly longer than the width of your belt. Now unfold the fabric, and refold it with the right side facing outward.

6 Thread red ribbon or string onto a large needle. Sew up the side of the leg, passing the needle through alternate holes. When you reach the top, sew back down through the empty holes to make a cross pattern. Tie the ribbon in place. Follow the steps again to make the second chaps leg. Wear them over trousers, and keep them up with a belt.

Gold watch

This antique-style watch can be slipped inside the pocket of a suit vest or the inner pocket of a jacket. It is the perfect prop for dressing up as an old-fashioned gentleman.

YOU WILL NEED

thick white foam board

compass and pencil

gold paint

purple paint

paintbrush

gold glitter pen

clear glue

brass eye

black map pin

black plastic container to make the watch hands

clear plastic container to make the hinge

thick gold thread

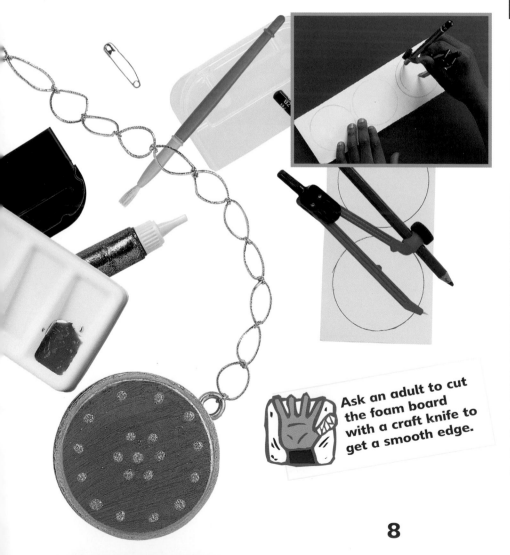

Ask an adult to cut the foam board with a craft knife to get a smooth edge.

1 Draw three circles the same size onto white foam board using a compass. Our circles each have a radius of 1½in (4cm).

2 Inside one circle, draw a slightly smaller circle to make a ring. Ask an adult to cut out the ring and two circles using a craft knife. Glue the ring on top of one circle.

8

3 The circle with the ring is the watch face. Paint the back, the sides, and the ring gold. Paint one side and the edges of the other circle gold, too. This is the watch cover.

4 Paint the face of the watch purple and the inside cover purple, too. Let the paint dry. Decorate the cover on either side with a pattern of gold glitter dots. Use the glitter pen to dot the 12 points of the watch face. Start with dots at 12 o'clock, 3 o'clock, 6 o'clock, and 9 o'clock, and then fill in two dots between them.

5 Screw a brass eye into the top of the watch back. Cut two clock hands out of black plastic, and attach them to the watch face using a map pin.

6 To make a hinge, cut a small rectangle out of clear plastic. Fold it in half, and glue it to the rim of the watch face. Let the glue dry. Glue the free end to the watch lid and leave to dry.

7 To make the watch chain, thread a length of gold string through the brass eye. Tie the two ends of the string together in knots, leaving gaps in between the knots.

Football helmet

Dress up as a star quarterback with this sturdy papier-mâché helmet. Make shoulder pads from cardboard to fit under your T-shirt. You could paint black stripes on your cheeks like a football player, too.

1 Blow up a balloon, and tie the neck. Place the balloon in a bowl, and attach it with tape to keep it steady. Mix up half PVA glue and half water in a bowl, and tear up strips of newspaper. Paste the strips all over the balloon. Let them dry. Then paste on two more layers of papier-mâché in this way, letting each layer dry.

YOU WILL NEED	
balloon	poster paints
newspaper	cable 20in (50cm) long
bowl	
masking tape	felt-tip pen
paintbrush	needle to make a hole
PVA glue	

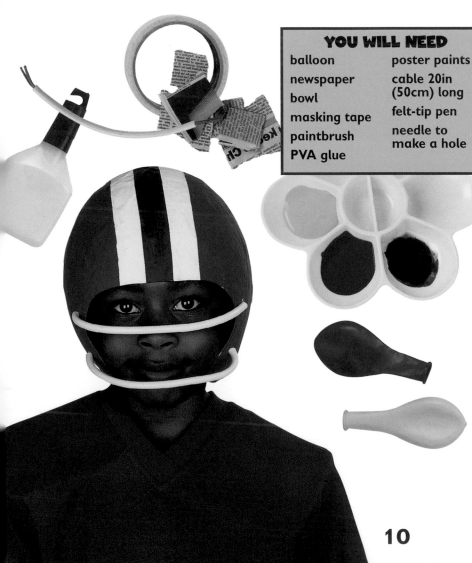

2 When the papier-mâché is dry, pop the balloon. Mark on the shape of the helmet. Cut out the helmet.

10

3 Paint the helmet all over with white poster paint. Let the paint dry.

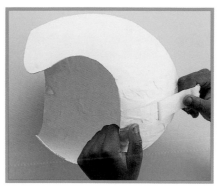

4 To make a neat stripe on the helmet, stick three lengths of masking tape onto the top of the helmet. They should stretch from the middle of the forehead to the back of the neck. The tape should be perfectly straight, each piece close up against the next. Now remove the middle strip of tape.

5 Paint along the middle stripe using blue paint. The tape will keep the stripe neat. Paint the sides of the helmet red. Let the paint dry, and then carefully remove the masking tape.

6 Make two holes on either side of the helmet using a darning needle. Ask an adult to cut two pieces of cable to fit across the helmet. He or she will need to trim the plastic coating from the ends of the cables using wire clippers. Push the wire through the holes in the helmet, and attach the ends inside using tape.

Ask an adult to cut the cable for you with wire clippers.

11

Treasure chest

This would be a great prop to go with the parrot you can make on page 26. Fill the chest with gold chocolate coins or old chains and jewelry that an adult can spare.

YOU WILL NEED

children's shoebox	paintbrush
corrugated cardboard	white, brown, and gold paint
masking tape	bathroom tissue
PVA glue	black marker pen
scissors	

1 Cut a strip of cardboard the same length as the shoebox lid and 2in (5cm) wider than the lid. Glue the cardboard strip to either side of the lid to make a curved top. We have used masking tape to keep the top in place while the glue dries.

2 Place one curved side onto cardboard and draw around it. Cut out two of these shapes. Tape them to the sides with long strips of masking tape. Snip tabs along the tape so that you can fold it down easily.

12

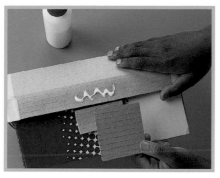

3 Fit the curved lid onto the shoebox. To make a lock, cut out two squares of corrugated cardboard. Fold one, and glue it in half. Glue it to the shoebox just under the lid. Glue the other square to the lid so that it hangs over the lock.

4 Paint the box and lid with white paint. This will cover up the patterns on the box and make a base coat. Let it dry. Paint the whole box with light-brown paint.

5 To add raised edges to the chest, first mix up half PVA glue and half water. Tear up bathroom tissue. Dip a brush into the paste and use it to push the tissue onto the chest. Build up a thick edge around the corners of the box and the lid. Let it dry.

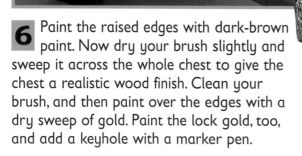

6 Paint the raised edges with dark-brown paint. Now dry your brush slightly and sweep it across the whole chest to give the chest a realistic wood finish. Clean your brush, and then paint over the edges with a dry sweep of gold. Paint the lock gold, too, and add a keyhole with a marker pen.

Spring bonnet

Dress up as a southern belle in this lovely pastel bonnet. We have used muslin, which is a light cotton fabric, but any light fabric will work well.

YOU WILL NEED

- large sheet of lilac cardboard
- pink muslin fabric about 3½ft x 2½ft (1m x 0.75m)
- scissors
- glue
- pencil
- gold glitter pen
- double-sided tape
- corrugated cardboard
- large round tray
- ruler

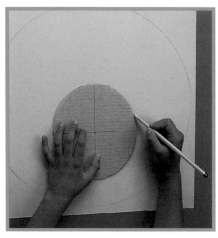

1 Draw a smooth oval onto corrugated cardboard, about the size of your head. Cut it out. Now draw a large circle onto lilac cardboard to make the brim of the bonnet. The best way to do this is to draw around a tray. Place the oval inside the brim toward the bottom, as shown. Draw around it.

2 Cut out the oval so you have a hole for your head in the bonnet.

14

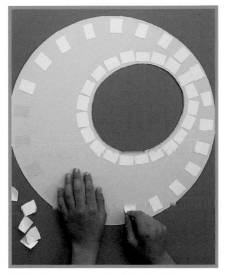

3 Cut out tabs of double-sided tape, and stick them all around the edges of the bonnet on one side.

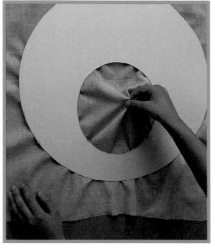

4 Lay the bonnet shape gently on top of a large piece of pink muslin, with the tape side down. Only press lightly so that the bonnet barely sticks to the fabric. Pull up the fabric inside the hole of the bonnet to a height of about 4in (10cm). Now press the cardboard firmly down onto the fabric so it sticks in place.

5 Trim the fabric around the edge of the bonnet, leaving a border about ½in (1cm) wide.

6 Decorate the border of the brim with a gold glitter pen. Let it dry. Cut a wide strip of muslin to tie around the bonnet and under your chin.

15

Sheriff's star

Make the chaps shown on page 6, tie a bandana around your neck, and add this silver badge to complete a Wild West sheriff's outfit.

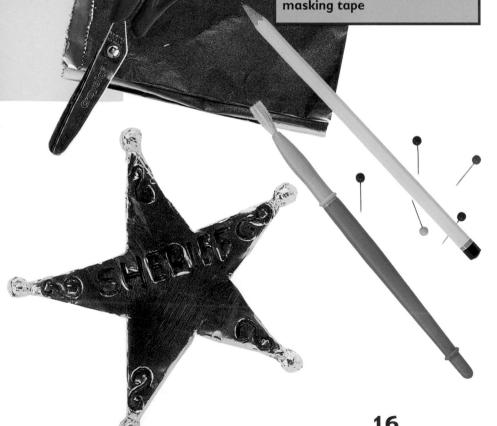

1 Trace the star and lettering on page 30. Transfer the star shape only onto thick white foam board, following the instructions on page 5.

2 Cut out the badge. To get smooth edges, you could ask an adult to cut the foam board using a craft knife.

16

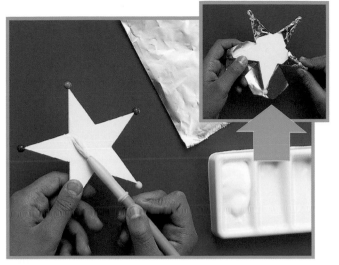

3 Stick a map pin into each point of the star. Paste glue over the badge, and cover it with a piece of kitchen foil. Smooth the foil with your fingers. Cut V shapes in the foil between the points of the star so you can fold it under.

4 Now put the tracing of the word "SHERIFF" on top of the badge. Go over it with a pencil, pressing firmly so that the word appears on the badge. Go over the letters with a ballpoint pen in red or black. Add twirls to the points of the badge.

5 Tape a safety pin to the back of the badge so that you can wear it.

Candy wrapper crown

Make this bejeweled crown out of foil wrappers. Start saving candy wrappers now so you have plenty of patterns and colors to choose from.

YOU WILL NEED

foil candy wrappers and shiny wrapping paper

glue

scissors

piece of scrap cardboard

strip of cardboard 29in x 8in (72cm x 20cm)

tracing paper

pencil

ruler

acrylic paint

paintbrush

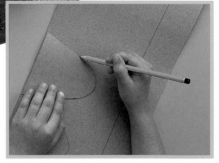

1 Take the strip of cardboard, and draw a line 2in (5cm) from the bottom. Now trace the rounded shape on page 30. Transfer the tracing onto scrap cardboard by following the instructions on page 5. Cut out the shape, and draw around it all the way along the top edge of the crown strip.

18

2 Cut out the curved shapes to make the points of the crown. Now cut off the long strip along the bottom. This will be a band to go around your crown.

3 Decorate the crown and the band with foil wrappers. Smear the cardboard with paper glue, and then press on squares of colored foil. You do not need to cover the crown right to the bottom because the band will cover it up.

4 Turn over the decorated pieces, and glue down the edges of the foil to make a neat finish. Paint the inside to make the whole crown look smart. Let the paint dry.

5 Glue the band along the bottom of the crown. Ask a friend to wrap the crown around your head and mark where you need to tape it so that it fits. If two points overlap, trim one and then tape the crown together.

19

Funky phones

Bleep, bleep, bleep. Make cell phones for you and a friend. Dress up for a fancy dress party, and spend time chattering on the phone.

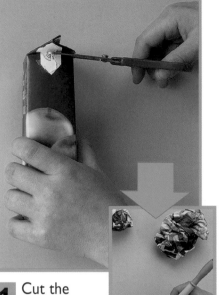

YOU WILL NEED

small juice carton	masking tape
scissors	cardboard
newspaper	craft foam
acrylic paint	black marker pen
paintbrush	glue

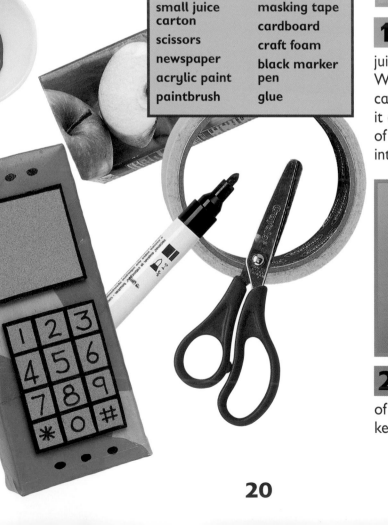

1 Cut the end off a juice carton. Wash out the carton, and let it dry. Then scrunch up pieces of newspaper, and push them into the carton.

2 When the carton is full of newspaper, tape a rectangle of cardboard over the end to keep in the paper.

3 Paint the phone with acrylic paints. Choose a few colors that are similar. For example, we have used pinks and purples. Or you could use different shades of green. We have painted on wiggles and blobs to make a camouflage pattern.

4 Cut a screen and a keypad out of craft foam. Draw the numbers, a star key, and a number key (#) on the keypad. Glue them onto your phone. Let the glue dry.

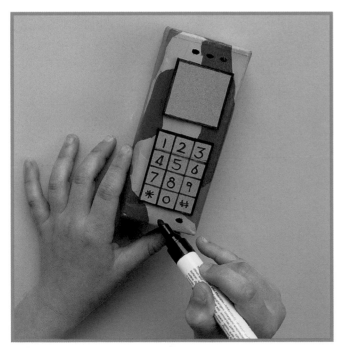

5 Decorate with a marker pen. Make a phone in different camouflage colors for your friend.

Bubblewrap wings

Hunt inside boxes for bubblewrap. Then you can make these wings for a bubbly butterfly. Why not make the butterfly antennas on page 28 to go with the wings?

1 Fold the sheet of bubblewrap in half along its longest side. Use a large plate to draw curved scallops from one corner on the edge to the diagonally opposite corner on the fold.

22

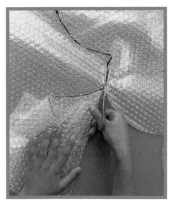

2 Cut out the wing shape along the curved lines, and unfold the wings.

3 Paint the bubble side of the wings with lime-green paint. Use a wide paintbrush.

4 You should have two leftover sections of bubblewrap. Paint one orange and one blue. Cut out two small circles and two medium-size circles from each colored sheet. Use the medium-size plate and the small bowl to draw around.

5 Place the colored circles on the wings around the edge. To attach the circles, cut pieces of glitter pipe cleaner 11⁄2in (4cm) long. Bend the ends to make them into staples. Push the glitter staples into the wings around each circle. Bend down the ends at the back. Make four holes in the wings along the top edge. Thread a piece of green ribbon through each hole. Now ask an adult to hold up the wings behind your back and tie the ribbons to your arms.

Flower garlands

In Hawaii these garlands or leis are symbols of friendship. Make lots so you and your friends can dress up as Hawaiian boys and girls.

YOU WILL NEED

pale-blue, cream, and green crêpe paper

pale green straws

string

scissors

green felt-tip pen

big needle

small roll of tape

pencil

1 Fold a piece of green crêpe paper in half and then in half again. Go on until you have a small square. Draw a circle onto the folded crêpe paper. You can use a small roll of tape to draw around.

2 Cut out the circle to make a stack of green crêpe circles. Cut circles in the pale-blue and cream crêpe paper.

24

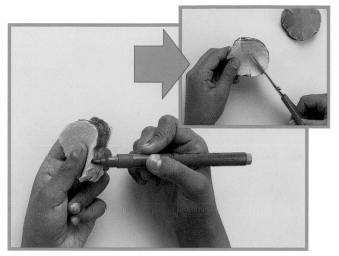

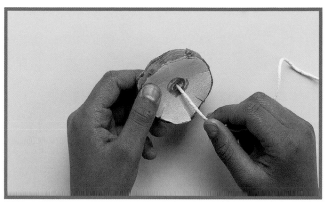

3 Use a green felt-tip pen to draw around the edge of the blue and cream circles. Make four snips around the edge to make petals. Draw on green centers, too. Make a hole in the center of the petals using a needle.

4 To make a flower, take a few pale-blue circles, and thread string through the center. Thread on a few green crêpe circles and then a few pale-blue circles. Cut up straws, and thread a small piece onto the string between each flower. Follow the blue flower with a cream flower.

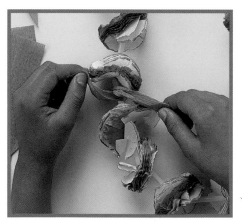

5 When you have finished the chain, tie the two ends of string together. To make leaves, cut thin strips of green crêpe paper about 12in (30cm) long, then cut them in half at an angle. Twist each strip in the middle, and tie one around each piece of straw.

25

Pirate's parrot

Every pirate needs a pet parrot. It is so easy to make and fits snugly on your shoulder. Look out for a bandana and an eye patch to complete the pirate costume.

YOU WILL NEED

corrugated cardboard
tracing paper
pencil
masking tape
glue
poster paints
paintbrush
scissors
newspaper
PVA glue
black marker pen

1 Trace the parrot on page 31. Transfer the tracing onto corrugated cardboard following the instructions on page 5.

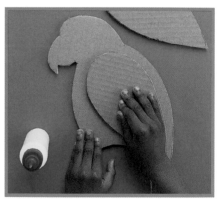

2 Cut out the parrot. Now transfer the wing shape onto a separate piece of cardboard, and cut it out. Cut out a second wing. Glue the wings to either side of the parrot's body.

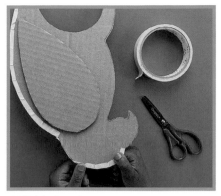

3 Make the edges smooth by sticking small lengths of masking tape all the way around the edge.

4 Mix up half PVA glue and half water in a bowl. Tear newspaper into strips, and paste them all over the parrot using the watery glue. Cover the whole parrot with two or three layers of papier-mâché in this way. Let it dry.

5 Paint the parrot using bright poster paints.

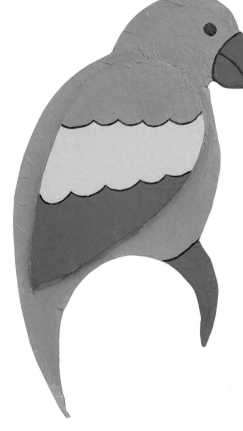

6 When the paint has dried, go over the features with a black marker pen.

Bouncy antennas

The butterfly antennas look cute with the butterfly wings you can make on page 22. Try making alien antennas as well, so you can dress up as a Martian or a Venusian.

1 For the butterfly antennas, wind an orange and a pink pipe cleaner around the hairband to one side. Twist the pipe cleaners together up to about halfway along.

2 Shape the ends to make a butterfly shape using the guideline on page 30, and then twist them together at the very top to make tiny antennas. Do the same on the other side of the hairband to make a second butterfly shape.

3 To make the alien antennas, wind a silver pipe cleaner around a thin stick. Then slip the stick out to leave the spiral antenna.

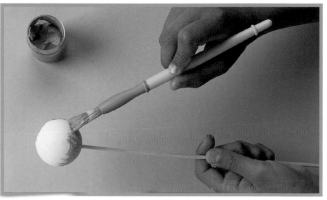

4 Ask an adult to make a hole in each Ping-Pong ball, using a darning needle. Paint the Ping-Pong balls green. To make it easier, push them onto a stick to hold them while you paint.

Ask an adult to make a hole in each Ping-Pong ball for you.

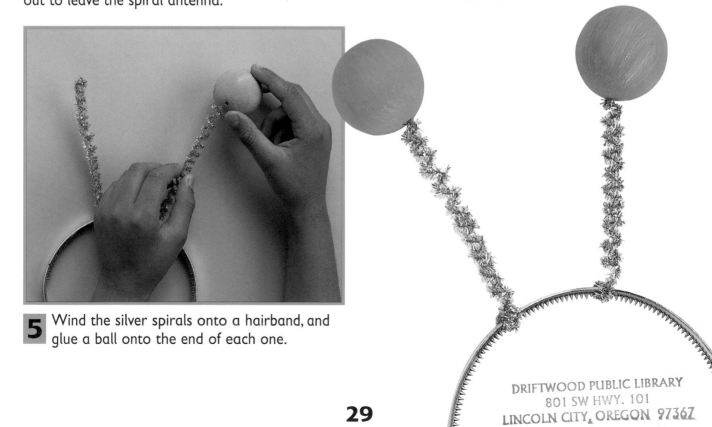

5 Wind the silver spirals onto a hairband, and glue a ball onto the end of each one.

Creative Crafts for Kids

Patterns

Here are the patterns you will need to make some of the projects. To find out how to make a pattern, follow the instructions in the "Making patterns" box on page 5. For some of the patterns you need to cut out two shapes. Transfer the tracing onto scrap paper, and cut out the paper template. Draw around the template to make as many shapes as you need.

Sheriff's star
page 16

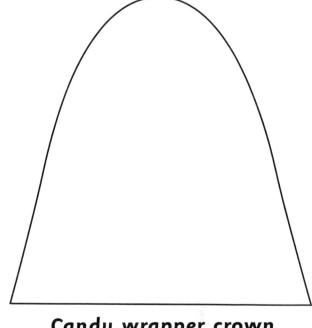

Candy wrapper crown
page 18

butterfly shape guideline

Bouncy antennas
page 28

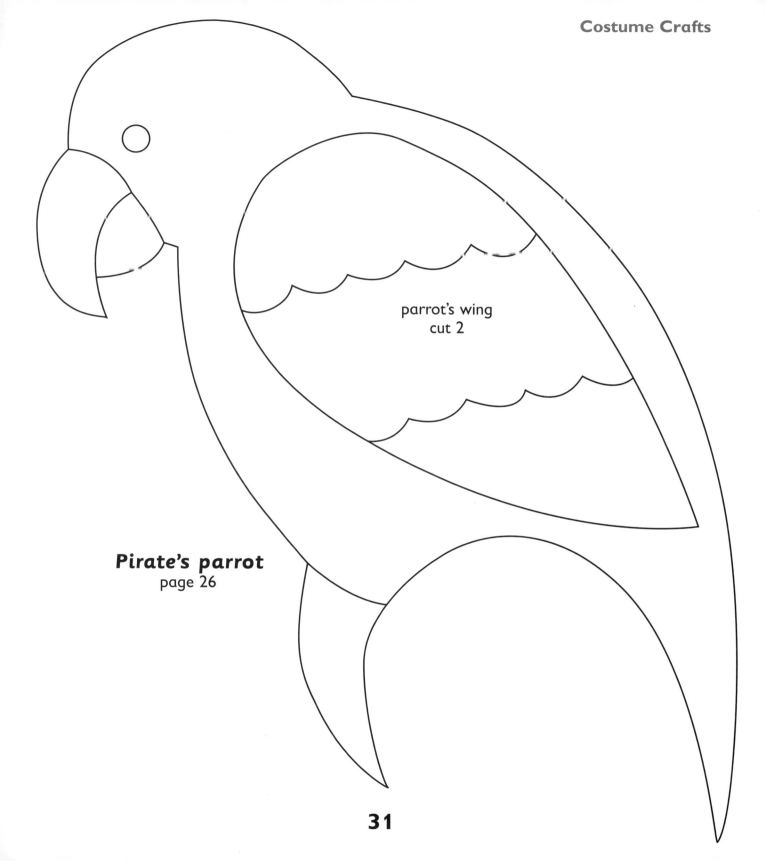

parrot's wing
cut 2

Pirate's parrot
page 26

Glossary

acrylic paint a paint, used especially for painting pictures, that is made with a manufactured acid

antenna a thin, rodlike organ used to feel things, located on the head of certain animals

antique an object that is valued because of its age

bandana a large square of cotton or silk worn over the hair or around the neck

bejeweled decorated with jewels or colorful objects

camouflage a color or pattern that matches the surroundings and helps hide something

chaps leather leggings worn over ordinary pants when riding horses

corrugated folded into parallel ridges

fringe a decorative border consisting of short strands of thread or other material

garland a wreath of connected flowers or leaves worn or used as decoration

hinge a movable joint used to fasten two things

muslin a thin, plain-weave cotton cloth used for curtains, sheets, and dresses

papier-mâché sheets of paper pulp and glue stuck together in layers, usually onto a mold, to make objects

PVA glue one of the most common glues. "PVA" stands for polyvinyl acetate.

Index